Ontario
ABCs

Jocey Asnong

RMB

All the animals
are awake

Algonquin National Park

B

Beavers brave the waves in the bay

Barrie

We call to each other
from the chairlift

Collingwood

D

Ducks dive for delicious treats

Duckbill Lake

We find fresh eggs at our farm

Elmira

Gulls gather for grilled lunch

Goderich

Huntsville

H

I

Hide inside our tree house

Jays sing a joyful song

Joyceville

Kingfisher keeps
an eye on us

Killarney Provincial Park

K

Listen to loons on the lake

M

Muskoka

Make a splash this morning

It's noisy near the waterfalls

Niagara Falls

O

ottawa

**Our skates go
fast outside**

Peek from behind pine trees

Pinery Provincial Park

A quest is better
with raccoons

Richmond Hill

Swans make a heart shape

Stratford

A tall tower touches the clouds

Toronto